The Bill Martin, Jr., Connection

with John Archambault

by Will C. Howell

FEARON TEACHER AIDS
Simon & Schuster Supplementary Education Group

Bill Martin, Jr.,

Thank you for your innovative teaching—showing educators and children how to play with language and to enjoy its sounds and shapes. And thank you for your inspiration—helping teachers and students rediscover curiosity, celebration, and hope.

John Archambault,

Thank you for joining the language celebration—merging your talent and sensitivity with Bill's to give us these wonderful children's books.

Will Howell

Editor: Carol Williams
Copyeditor: Kristin Eclov
Illustration: Gwen Connelly
Cover illustration: Ted Rand
Design: Diann Abbott

ISBN 0-86653-991-3

Printed in the United States of America
1. 9 8 7 6 5 4 3 2

Contents

Introduction

The emphasis on "The Year of the Young Reader" (1989) and "International Literacy Year" (1990) has helped children's literature come of age. Research confirms that good reading and writing are best taught by using good books. And today, educators are fortunate to have a wide selection of excellent children's books to choose from.

The Bill Martin, Jr., Connection is written for librarians and teachers who want to effectively use good literature in their classrooms. The lessons present art, math, creative writing, science, and social studies activities to accompany books written by Bill Martin, Jr., and John Archambault. The variety of interdisciplinary activities and the whole-language instructional approach incorporated in the lessons will help you meet the diverse needs and interests of your students.

As students become familiar with various works by a single author, they develop an ability to analyze literary and artistic styles. The students can go to the library and select books written or illustrated by authors they feel as if they have actually met. "Connecting" with authors stimulates students to become involved in and enthusiastic about reading, writing, and learning. *The Bill Martin, Jr., Connection* gives students the opportunity to meet the author of the classic *Brown Bear, Brown Bear, What Do You See?* and other popular books.

Lessons require minimal preparation, while resulting in maximum participation and learning. A brief synopsis of each book is included. Read the book aloud to the children and invite them to enjoy the illustrations before participating in the activities. Exciting activities, including Milk Bucket Measuring, Pumpkin Picking, and Butterfly Art, will help you to enhance and reinforce your curriculum.

Meet Bill Martin, Jr.

Bill Martin, Jr., was born on March 20, 1916.

Bill grew up in the small town of Hiawatha, Kansas, where an emotional disturbance kept him from learning to read. Although Bill was unable to read a complete sentence or listen to a complete paragraph read aloud, he developed a love of the sound of language through his grandmother's storytelling.

Bill did not read a complete book until he was twenty years old and a student at Emporia State University in Kansas. Fortunately, at that time, he did not need to take an entrance exam to begin his studies at the university.

In college, Bill discovered his talent for writing. One of Bill's professors told him that to be a good writer one must also be a reader.

Bill went on to attend graduate school, became a teacher, and eventually an elementary school principal. He then joined Holt, Rinehart and Winston and collaborated on the popular *Sounds of Language* reading series.

Little Squeegy Bug, Bill Martin's first book, sold over a million copies. In the 1970s, Bill Martin, Jr., collaborated with fellow authors to publish a series of hardcover books. These small books were designed to fit easily into a child's hand and the text was simple and repetitive. In the 1980s, John Archambault joined Bill in creating many delightful new trade books for children. *White Dynamite and Curly Kidd* was listed on the School Library Journal of Best Books in 1986 and *Knots on a Counting Rope* made the same list in 1987. *Knots on a Counting Rope* and *Barn Dance* have also been featured on the television program *The Reading Rainbow.*

Bill Martin, Jr., writes to help children discover the marvel of the sound of language and the miracle of the shape of print. He fills his books with celebration, courage, and hope.

Meet John Archambault

John Archambault received his B.A. from the University of California in 1981. He also attended Columbia Teacher's College. He is a poet and a journalist.

Once, while giving Bill Martin, Jr., a ride to the airport, John and Bill got to talking about poetry and writing. A partnership took seed, and from this relationship has grown a collaboration producing many wonderful picture books for children.

Both authors bring memories from their childhood to their writing. John recalls growing up in Pasadena, California, and a particularly "deep ravine with a large sprawling oak tree reaching out in seemingly every direction." That memory and one of Bill's memories of picking up milk in a bucket from a farmer at the edge of town led to a reader's theater performance and finally to the book *The Ghost-Eye Tree*.

John's favorite book as a child was *Charlotte's Web*. The love of lively language and dialog that John experienced in his early reading carries over into his own writing with Bill Martin, Jr.

Barn Dance!

Everyone is asleep, except the skinny kid. The night owl beckons him to "come a little closer" and experience the magic in the air. The magic begins as the scarecrow starts a-fiddlin'. The text swings the reader into the rhythm of the story and the wonder of words. Ted Rand's illustrations capture the enchantment of the midnight barn dance.

Written by Bill Martin, Jr., and
John Archambault
Illustrated by Ted Rand
New York: Henry Holt, 1986

❧ • WRITING A LIST • ❧

Materials:

• worksheet on page 11
• pencils

Lesson Procedure

1. Discuss what the author meant when he described the boy as "the skinny kid with questions in his head." Ask children what kinds of questions the skinny boy might have had in his mind.
2. Ask students if they have questions in their heads. Ask students if they are curious about what is going on around them or if there are things they wish they knew more about. Stimulate students with thought-provoking questions encouraging their curious minds to wonder.
3. Invite students to write down some of their own questions on the worksheet.
4. Suggest that students keep the list of questions in a writing folder. The questions are a good source of writing or research ideas.

Taking It Further . . .

Students can use the worksheet to create a list of questions about a book they have just finished reading. Invite students to write questions about the characters, the ending of the story, or possible future outcomes.

Barn Dance!

Questions in My Head

Make a list of questions you would like to have answered.

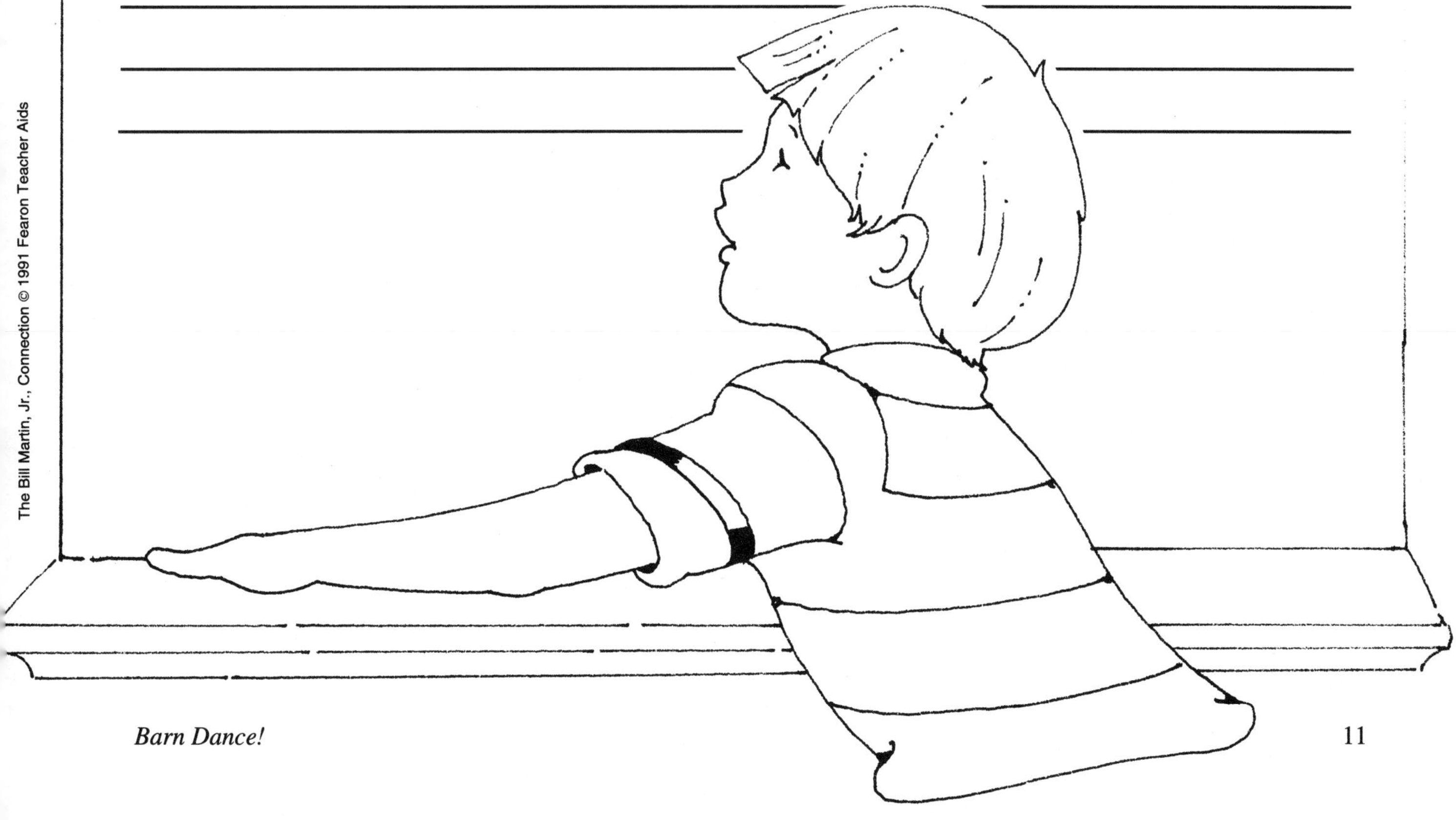

_____

_____

_____

_____

_____

_____

_____

_____

_____

_____

_____

_____

The Bill Martin, Jr., Connection © 1991 Fearon Teacher Aids

CREATIVE WRITING

Materials:

- •magazine pictures of sleeping animals
- •lined paper
- •pencils
- •glue

Lesson Procedure

1. Show children the picture of the sleeping ol' houn' dog in the story. The author described what the sleeping dog was dreaming about. Ask children what other dreams a dog might have.
2. Give each child a sheet of lined paper and a magazine picture of a sleeping animal.
3. Encourage students to write a poem, paragraph, or short story about what the animal in their pictures might be dreaming about. Students can glue the animal pictures on the lined paper to enhance their dream descriptions.

Taking It Further . . .

Encourage students to write or tell about a dream they have had. Students can share a fantasy or daydream they often think about as well.

VOCABULARY

Materials:

- worksheet on page 14
- dictionaries and encyclopedias
- pencils

Lesson Procedure

1. Discuss and define the square dance terms mentioned in the story.

   do-si-do   rocket to the moon   hurry home to mama
   curtsey   powderpuff your noses

2. Give each student a worksheet and discuss the terms listed.
3. Encourage students to use dictionaries and encyclopedias to define the unfamiliar dance terms. Provide definitions for the terms students are unable to locate.

Allemande—a one-hand turn done by grasping the partner's hand with thumbs up

Arch—two people face each other, join hands, and raise their arms to allow other dancers to pass through

Chassé—a sideways step executed by stepping out with one foot and then bringing the feet together

Circle Left—dancers join hands and rotate clockwise

Cross—a dancer changes places with the person across from him or her, passing right shoulders

Do-si-do—two dancers step around each other, back-to-back, with arms folded on chest

Grand Chain—a dancer gives his or her right hand to a partner and passes by and then extends left hand to the next partner and passes by, repeating the pattern

Honor Your Partner—a dancer bows or curtsies to his or her partner

Neighbor—the dancer standing next to you on the opposite side than your partner

Partner—a girl's partner is the boy on her left and a boy's partner is the girl on his right

Taking It Further . . .

Invite a square dancer or caller to the classroom to demonstrate some dance steps. Encourage students to join in and try the steps as well. Invite students to make up their own dance terms and illustrate them.

Square Dance Vocabulary

Define each dance term.

1. Allemande _____

_____

_____

2. Arch _____

3. Chassé _____

_____

4. Circle Left _____

_____

5. Cross _____

_____

6. Do-si-do _____

_____

7. Grand Chain _____

_____

8. Honor Your Partner _____

_____

9. Neighbor _____

_____

10. Partner _____

_____

The Bill Martin, Jr., Connection © 1991 Fearon Teacher Aids

Barn Dance!

❧ • QUILT PATTERNS • ☙

Materials:

- •worksheet on page 16
- •colored pencils, crayons, markers, or paint
- •pencils

Lesson Procedure

1. Show children the picture of the quilt on the skinny boy's bed at the beginning and ending of the story.
2. Discuss the pattern in the quilt. Ask students to describe the pattern on a quilt or blanket they have at home.
3. Give each student a worksheet and invite students to sketch a quilt pattern. Emphasize repetition, balance, and design.
4. After the sketch is complete, invite students to plan a color scheme and color their quilts. Again, emphasize repetition and balance when coloring the designs.
5. Backed with complementary-colored construction paper, display the quilt designs on a bulletin board to make an attractive display.

Taking It Further . . .

Ask parents to send in quilts for a class quilt show or find a volunteer to demonstrate quilting techniques. The class could also design a quilt to illustrate *Barn Dance!* Each child could design a quilt square portraying one part of the story.

Design your own quilt pattern. Sketch your design with pencil and then color the patterns.

The Bill Martin, Jr., Connection © 1991 Fearon Teacher Aids

Brown Bear, Brown Bear,

The simple, straightforward text in this story draws early readers into its playful pattern. Like the text, the bold illustrations are free of distracting details. This book is a masterpiece of language and color in its purest form.

Written by Bill Martin, Jr.
Illustrated by Eric Carle
New York: Henry Holt, 1983

What Do You See?

SEQUENCING

Materials:

•squares of colored construction paper

Lesson Procedure

1. Discuss the sequence of the animals mentioned in the story. Use the color strips on the inside front or back cover of the book as an outline.

brown bear	blue horse	white dog
red bird	green frog	black sheep
yellow duck	purple cat	

2. Place a construction-paper square on the floor to represent each animal. Mix the squares and ask students to put them back in order.
3. Divide the class into groups of 4-6. Encourage the children to retell the story using the colored squares as clues. After a bit of practice, invite students to retell the story without the help of visual clues.

Taking It Further . . .

Organize the students into several groups of six students each. Give each group a set of construction-paper squares (pink, orange, gray, lavender, turquoise, and tan). Distribute one square to each group member. Explain to students that they will be creating original stories based on the colored squares. Each student in the group will be responsible for contributing one part of the story based on the colored square he or she receives. For example, the student holding the pink square could begin the story by saying, "Once upon a time, there was a pink ballerina. She had only one shoe." After the student has had one minute, the story passes to the student holding the orange square who might say, "The pink ballerina went to the store to buy another shoe. There she met a man in an orange shirt." The story continues until each student has had one minute to add his or her colorful contribution. After the entire story has been told, ask for a volunteer from the group to retell the entire story using the colored squares as clues.

Brown Bear, Brown Bear, What Do You See?

❧ • TELLING TIME • ☙

Materials:

- worksheet on page 20
- pencils

Lesson Procedure

1. Apply the question and answer pattern of the story to a math lesson about telling time.
2. Make a copy of the worksheet on page 20. Draw hands on each clock before duplicating it for students. (Do *not* write the times below each clock.)
3. Give each child a copy of the worksheet. Begin with the first clock and ask a student what time the clock says. For example, "Robert, Robert, what time do you see?" Robert would answer by saying, "I see 2:30, that's what I see."
4. After the student answers correctly, write the time on the chalkboard. Students can write the time below the clock on their papers.
5. Continue asking the question and calling on a student to answer until the worksheet is completed.

Taking It Further . . .

Practice cardinal numbers by asking students to name and count body parts on each animal from the story. For example, there is *one* bear and he has *five* toes and *two* ears. Practice ordinal numbers by asking students in which order the animals appeared in the story. For example, the bear was *first* and the horse was *fourth*.

What Time Is It?

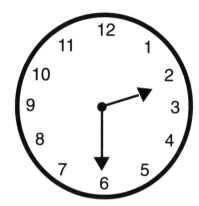

1. ___ **2:30** ___

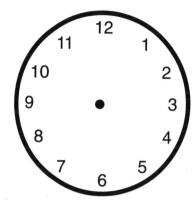

2. _____

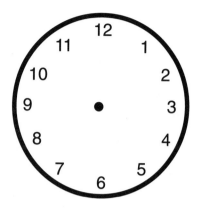

3. _____

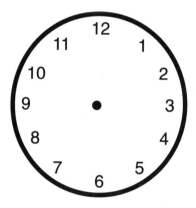

4. _____

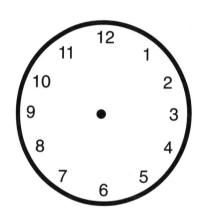

5. _____

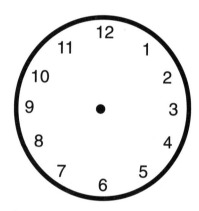

6. _____

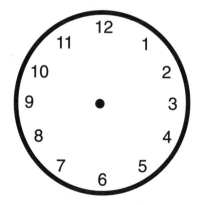

7. _____

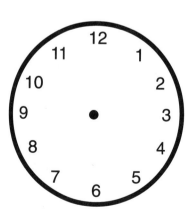

8. _____

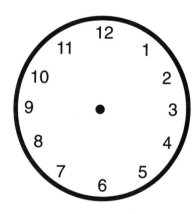

9. _____

Brown Bear, Brown Bear, What Do You See?

The Bill Martin, Jr., Connection © 1991 Fearon Teacher Aids

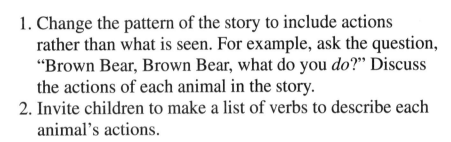

• ANIMAL ACTIONS •

Materials:

• worksheet on page 22
• pencils

Lesson Procedure

1. Change the pattern of the story to include actions rather than what is seen. For example, ask the question, "Brown Bear, Brown Bear, what do you *do*?" Discuss the actions of each animal in the story.
2. Invite children to make a list of verbs to describe each animal's actions.

Bear	Duck	Bird
see	see	see
growl	swim	fly
fish	dive	hatch

3. Encourage children to share their lists with the class.

Taking It Further . . .

Encourage students to use their lists as "verb banks" for creative writing.

Name _____

Brown Bear, Brown Bear, What Do You Do?

Write a list of verbs (action words) to describe what each animal can do.

Bear	**Horse**	**Dog**
_____	_____	_____
_____	_____	_____
_____	_____	_____
_____	_____	_____

Bird	**Frog**	**Sheep**
_____	_____	_____
_____	_____	_____
_____	_____	_____
_____	_____	_____

Duck	**Cat**	**Fish**
_____	_____	_____
_____	_____	_____
_____	_____	_____
_____	_____	_____

The Bill Martin, Jr., Connection © 1991 Fearon Teacher Aids

Brown Bear, Brown Bear, What Do You See?

COLOR WHEELS

Materials:

- •worksheet on page 24
- •paper plates
- •scissors
- •crayons or markers
- •glue
- •pencils

Lesson Procedure

1. Invite students to color each animal on the worksheet the same color each animal is in the story. Have students cut out the animals on the worksheet.
2. Give each child a paper plate and ask children to use a pencil to divide the plate into thirds. Explain to children that the dividing lines on the plate will look very similar to the letter *Y*.
3. Explain to the students that red, yellow, and blue are called *primary* colors. Have students glue a primary-colored animal in each section of the paper plate—one animal per section (red bird, yellow duck, and blue horse).
4. Explain to the students that orange, green, and purple are called *secondary* colors. Secondary colors can be made by mixing two primary colors. Have students glue the secondary-colored animals on the paper plate between the primary-colored animals. Students can glue each animal between the two primary colors that would make that animal's color when mixed. For example, a gold fish (orange) would be glued between a red bird and a yellow duck.

Taking It Further . . .

Students can experiment with texture by creating each animal mentioned in the story using different materials.

bear—sandpaper	horse—aluminum foil	cat—tissue paper	fish—confetti
bird—felt	frog—leaf	sheep—steel wool	dog—tracing paper
duck—satin			

Name _____

Color each animal the color it is in the story.

Brown Bear, Brown Bear, What Do You See?

Chicka Chicka

This alphabet book has a rhythm that will hit with a BOOM! It's a chant that demands to be read aloud again and again. The bright, bold colors make the story a festival of fun for everyone.

Written by Bill Martin, Jr., and John Archambault
Illustrated by Lois Ehlert
New York: Simon & Schuster, 1989

Boom Boom

❧ CHORAL READING ❧

Materials:

Lesson Procedure

1. After reading the story aloud to the class once, invite students to participate as you read it a second time.
2. Divide the class into three groups. Assign each group a repetitive line from the story to say along with you as you read the story.

   Group 1: "The coconut tree" (encourage a calypso rhythm)
   Group 2: "Chicka chicka" (encourage children to emphasize the "ch" sound by thinking of the sound a train makes as it chugs down the tracks)
   Group 3: "Boom boom!" (encourage children to think of a cannon firing)

3. As you read the story a second time, orchestrate each group to recite its part at the correct time.

Taking It Further . . .

Assign each child a letter of the alphabet to fill in as the story is read aloud again.

❧ • ALPHABETIZING • ❧

Materials:

•3" x 5" cards

Lesson Procedure

1. Choose several spelling or vocabulary words and write one on each 3" x 5" card.
2. As a class, put the cards in alphabetical order.
3. Encourage children to read a word card to substitute for each letter mentioned as you reread the story.
4. For example, if vocabulary words from *Barn Dance!* were chosen, the first page of the story might read like this:

> "*Curtsey* told *Faint*,
> and *Faint* told *Hoedown*,
> I'll meet you at the top
> of the coconut tree."

Taking It Further . . .

Design a coconut tree bulletin-board display. Make a tall brown trunk with large green fronds. Title the bulletin board "The Alphabet Tree." Use a list of words you are currently studying (spelling, science vocabulary, reading) and write them on colorful squares of construction paper. Glue each colorful square to a brown construction-paper coconut. Students can help staple the coconuts to the tree so the words are in alphabetical order.

❧ • SCRAMBLED WORDS • ❧

Materials:

- worksheet on page 29
- pencils

Lesson Procedure

1. Remind the students how the alphabet letters tumbled from the coconut tree and were then all mixed-up on the ground.
2. Give each student a copy of the worksheet and invite children to unscramble each mixed-up word from the story.
3. Students write the unscrambled word on the line next to its scrambled partner.

1. mobo-boom	8. wond-down	15. herit-their
2. ared-dare	9. anut-aunt	16. helow-whole
3. reet-tree	10. tonk-knot	17. celnu-uncle
4. reef-free	11. stud-dust	18. gelant-tangle
5. neek-knee	12. leph-help	19. utocnoc-coconut
6. nomo-moon	13. sw700-twist	20. plabathe-alphabet
7. tabe-beat	14. phact-patch	

Taking It Further . . .

Encourage students to make their own list of scrambled words to exchange with a partner. The list might include vocabulary words from a unit of study, spelling words, verbs, adjectives, or animal words. To make the task of unscrambling easier for younger children, underline or circle the letter each unscrambled word begins with.

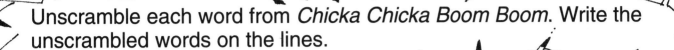

Scrambled Words

Unscramble each word from *Chicka Chicka Boom Boom*. Write the unscrambled words on the lines.

1. mobo _____
2. ared _____
3. reet _____
4. reef _____
5. neek _____
6. nomo _____
7. tabe _____
8. wond _____
9. anut _____
10. tonk _____
11. stud _____
12. leph _____
13. switt _____
14. phact _____
15. herit _____
16. helow _____
17. celnu _____
18. gelant _____
19. utocnoc _____
20. plabathe _____

Chicka Chicka Boom Boom

CREATIVE WRITING

Materials:

- letters cut from magazines
- scissors
- glue
- drawing paper
- lined paper
- pencils

Lesson Procedure

1. Invite each student to select a favorite letter of the alphabet.
2. Students glue their letters to a sheet of drawing paper and then draw a picture incorporating the letter as part of the illustration.
3. Encourage students to write short stories or paragraphs about their illustrations on lined paper.

Taking It Further . . .

Reread the last two pages of the story. Discuss what might happen after "A" states his dare, "Dare double dare, you can't catch me. I'll beat you to the top of the coconut tree." Encourage students to write stories about the events that might follow if the story continued.

COUNTING

Materials:

Lesson Procedure

1. Explain to students that they will be helping to change the story from an alphabet book to a counting book.
2. Begin reading the story and invite children to fill in numbers to replace the letters.

> "1 told 2,
> and 2 told 3,
> I'll meet you at the top
> of the coconut tree."

Taking It Further . . .

Before beginning the activity, ask children to predict how many numbers will be used in the story (26). Practice some math calculations by asking students such questions as "If 4, 5, and 6 are all in the coconut tree, what is the total?" "If 7 joins them, what will the total be then?"

◆ LETTER COLLAGE ◆

Materials:

• worksheet on page 33
• old magazines
• scissors
• glue

Lesson Procedure

1. Divide the class into several groups. Give each child a copy of the worksheet and each group of children a supply of magazines.
2. Invite children to cut alphabet letters from the magazines and glue the letters on the worksheet to create a coconut tree letter collage.
3. Encourage students to be creative by adding color using crayons or markers or making a border using confetti.

Taking It Further . . .

Encourage students to create their own collage ideas on sheets of drawing paper. Students can use the letters in their names, vowels, or make a collage using different sizes and styles of only one letter.

Coconut Tree Letter Collage

Cut letters from a magazine.
Glue the letters on the coconut tree.

The Ghost-Eye

A young boy and his older sister confront their fear of running an errand for their mother in the dark night. The two children take the reader along with them as they embark on their journey past an eerie old tree. The rhythm and suspense quickly pull the reader into the story.

Written by Bill Martin, Jr., and
John Archambault
Illustrated by Ted Rand
New York: Henry Holt, 1985

Tree

❧ • CREATIVE WRITING • ❧

Materials:

- hats
- lined paper
- pencils

Lesson Procedure

1. Remind children how the little boy enjoyed wearing his hat and took extra care to be sure he had it on when he went on the errand for his mother.
2. Encourage each student to wear an interesting hat to school. Have a few extra hats available for children who are unable to bring hats of their own. Invite children to make hats to wear for the assignment. *Hats, Hats and More Hats!* by Jean Stangl (Fearon Teacher Aids, 1989) is an excellent resource.
3. Invite students to write a short story or paragraph about the hats they are wearing. Encourage students to include a detailed description of the hat, the way they feel when they are wearing it, where they got the hat, and why it is so special to them.
4. Students can share their stories with the class.

Taking It Further . . .

Invite students to imagine what it would be like to participate in a sleep-out under the Ghost-Eye Tree. Encourage students to write stories about their nighttime adventures. Emphasize the use of descriptive words, actions, and sounds to create an eerie mood.

❦ • MILK BUCKET MEASURING • ❧

Materials:

• worksheet on page 38
• pencils

Lesson Procedure

1. Remind students of the milk bucket and how the milk was spilled.
2. Ask the students to guess how much milk they think the bucket can hold (probably about three gallons).
3. Give a worksheet to each student and invite children to answer each question.

Answers to Worksheet
1. 2 gallons
2. 6 quarts
3. 4 days
4. 13 cups, or 6 pints and 1 cup, or 3 quarts and 1 cup
5. 16 oz, 32 oz, 128 oz
6. $21.00
7. 12 cups, or 6 pints, or 3 quarts
8. 6 quarts

4. After students have completed the worksheet, invite them to create an original story problem on the back. Encourage children to exchange papers and solve a neighbor's problem.

Taking It Further . . .

Set up a learning center for students to experience hands-on practice measuring liquids. Provide a milk bucket, assorted jars (pint, quart, gallon), and water. Invite students to fill containers, transfer the liquid, and write equivalent equations based on their experimentation.

Milk Bucket Measuring

2 cups = 1 pint   4 quarts = 1 gallon
2 pints = 1 quart   3 gallons = 1 bucket

1. If the bucket were full of milk and the children spilled one-third of the milk on the way home, how many gallons of milk would be left? _____

2. If the children spilled one-half of the full bucket of milk on the way home, how many quarts of milk would be left? _____

3. If the boy, his sister, and their mother each drink 4 cups of milk a day, how long will it take them to drink a bucket of milk?

   _____

4. Mother used 3 pints of milk to make yogurt, 2 cups of milk to make pudding, and 1 quart of milk to make chowder. She gave 1 cup of milk to the cat. How much milk did Mother use?

   _____

5. If there are 8 ounces in a cup of milk, how many ounces are there in a pint? _____ a quart? _____ a gallon?_____

6. Mr. Cowlander sold 7 buckets of milk. If he charged $3.00 a bucket, how much did Mr. Cowlander earn? _____

7. The cat and her kittens drank 5 cups of milk from the bucket when it was sitting on the step. There were 7 cups of milk left in the bucket after they finished drinking. How much milk was in the bucket before the cats came along? _____

8. It took 6 quarts of water to fill the bucket after the children had spilled some of the milk. How much milk was in the bucket before the children filled it with water? _____

The Ghost-Eye Tree

HANDLING FEAR

Materials:

•worksheet on page 40
•pencils

Lesson Procedure

1. Discuss how fear affected the characters in the story. Discuss the characters' feelings and actions (they ran, spilled the bucket of milk, got edgy with each other).
2. Discuss ways people handle fear. Ask students to explain feelings of fear they have experienced and how the feelings affected their actions.
3. Give each child a copy of the worksheet and invite children to list the ways they handle fear.
4. Discuss the students' suggestions on handling fear. Make a composite list of ideas on the chalkboard.

Taking It Further . . .

Remind the children of what the characters in the story feared. Ask children if they would have been afraid in the same situation. Invite students to make a list of things or situations that scare them. Encourage each child to choose one specific fear from the list and then help each child come up with a constructive way of dealing with it.

The Ghost-Eye Tree

Name _____

Make a list of things you do when you are afraid.

The Ghost-Eye Tree

The Bill Martin, Jr., Connection © 1991 Fearon Teacher Aids

❦ • PAINT AND CHALK • ❦

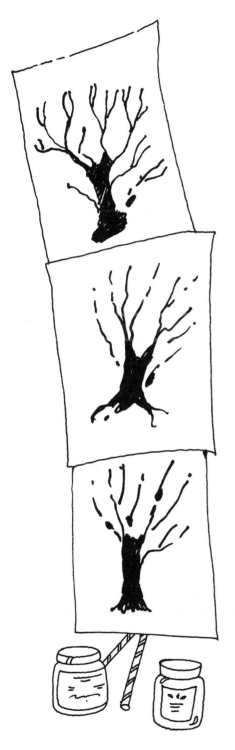

Materials:

• fingerpaint paper
• blue or gray fingerpaint
• black tempera paint
• straws
• chalk

Lesson Procedure

1. Invite students to make an eerie, blue or gray background design by spreading fingerpaint on the entire piece of fingerpaint paper. Allow the paint to dry.
2. Place a small amount of black paint on each child's dried background at the spot where the child would like the base of a tree to begin.
3. Give each child a straw. Children spread the black paint upwards by blowing gently through the straw into the paint. The paint will be blown upwards on the paper to make an interesting tree shape.
4. After the paint has dried, children can use chalk to draw a moon and spooky eyes.

Taking It Further . . .

Cover a bulletin board with blue or gray background paper. Divide the class into groups to make trees, houses, story characters, cats, and other details from *The Ghost-Eye Tree*. Display student creations. Invite a group of students to cut letters from construction paper for the book title.

Here Are My

Young children will enjoy acting out this rhythmic book about hands, feet, and other body parts. The multicultural characters help create a sense of world community and remind children of the similarities we all share.

Written by Bill Martin, Jr., and
John Archambault
Illustrated by Ted Rand
New York: Henry Holt, 1985

Hands

❧ • CREATIVE WRITING • ❧

Materials:

- worksheets on pages 45-46
- pencils
- hole punch
- four binder rings
- scissors

Lesson Procedure

1. Ask children to name as many things as possible that they can do with their hands (clap, pet an animal, shake a friend's hand, pour a glass of milk).
2. After generating ideas, give each student a copy of the hand worksheet. Invite children to write several sentences describing things their hands can do. Invite younger children to copy sentences from the chalkboard based on oral discussion.
3. Have each child cut out the handprint on the worksheet. Punch holes where indicated and combine all the hands together to make a class booklet. Use two binder rings to hold the booklet together.
4. Repeat the same lesson on another day using the foot worksheet on page 46. Make a class foot booklet.

Taking It Further . . .

Invite children to write a story or paragraph entitled "A Day in the Life of My Hand" or "A Day in the Life of My Foot."

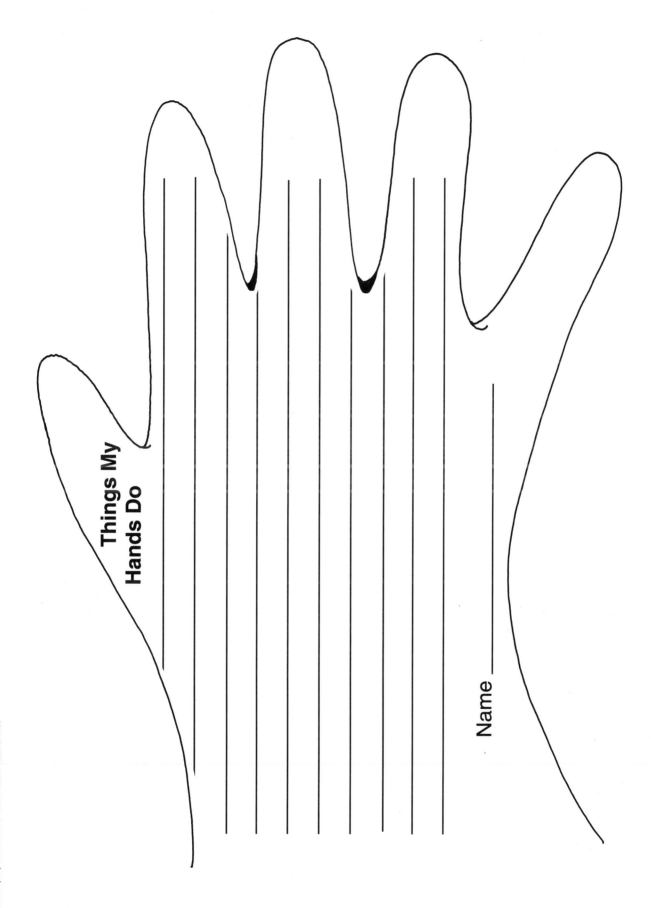

Things My Hands Do

Name _____

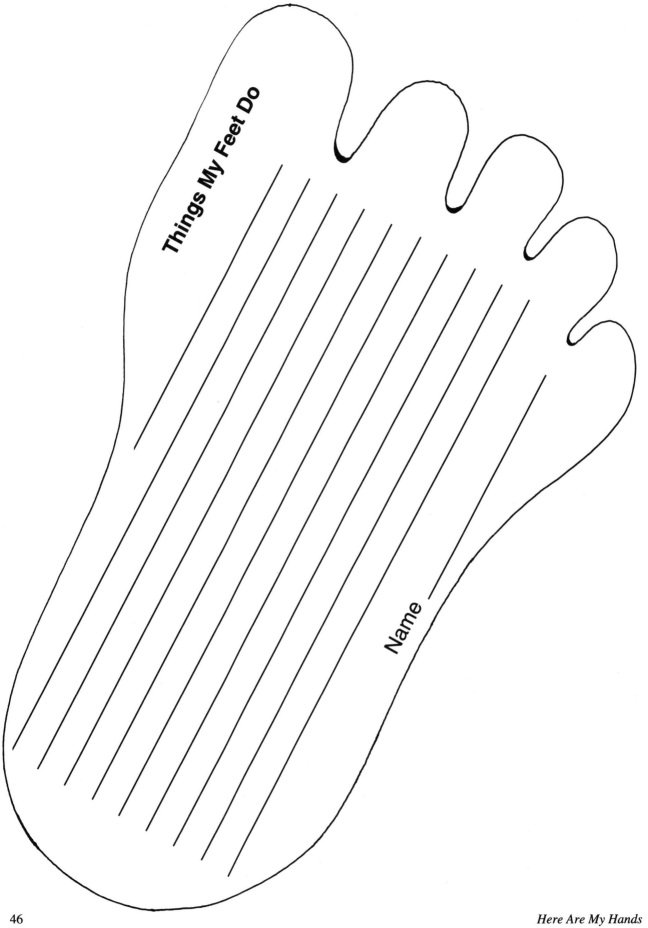

Things My Feet Do

Name

The Bill Martin, Jr., Connection © 1991 Fearon Teacher Aids

Here Are My Hands

☙ • EYES OF THE WORLD • ☙

Materials:

- worksheet on page 48
- travel brochures and old magazines
- scissors
- glue

Lesson Procedure

1. Show children the picture from the story of the child making eyeglass frames with his fingers around his eyes. Ask children in what part of the world they think this child might live and why.
2. Ask children to name some things they enjoy seeing with their eyes. Ask students if they think children who live in other parts of the world enjoy seeing the same things.
3. Remind students that although there are different things to see and enjoy in various parts of the world, there are also similar things as well. Explain to students that people everywhere enjoy looking at the same moon, sun, and stars. Ask children to name other things that everyone in the world sees and enjoys.
4. Invite students to write a list, in the space provided, of things children all over the world enjoy seeing.

Taking It Further . . .

Give each child a copy of the worksheet on page 48. Encourage children to cut out pictures from magazines or travel brochures of children or people from various parts of the world. Have children glue the people across the top of the worksheet.

Name _____

What Do All the Children See?

_____
_____
_____
_____
_____
_____
_____

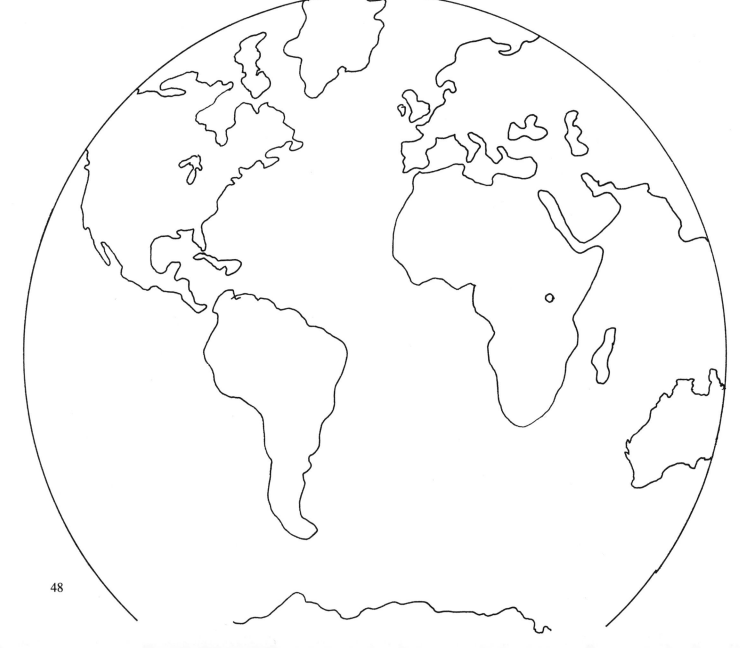

❧ • MYSTERY PRINTS • ❧

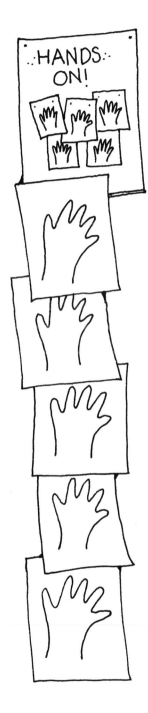

Materials:

- •construction paper
- •pencils
- •scissors

Lesson Procedure

1. Give each child a sheet of construction paper and invite students to trace and cut out one of their hand-prints.
2. Have students write their names on the back of the handprints.
3. Mount the handprints on a bulletin board with the names concealed. Label each handprint with a number.
4. Invite students to guess which handprint belongs to which student. Discuss the many ways each person is unique.
5. Repeat the activity using footprints. Have children trace and cut out a print of one of their bare feet.
6. This activity makes an excellent Open House display. Parents enjoy trying to identify their own child's hand or footprint.

Taking It Further . . .

Rather than tracing the prints with pencil, make hand or footprints with paint. Children place their hands or feet in a shallow dish of tempera paint and then carefully place them on clean sheets of drawing paper.

BODY OWNER'S MANUAL

Materials:

- •lined paper
- •drawing paper
- •pencils

Lesson Procedure

1. Discuss the importance of proper care of our bodies. Invite students to share some of their own daily health habits.
2. Divide the class into groups and assign each group a body part that needs care. Encourage group members to design a chapter of the *Body Owner's Manual* for their body part. For example,

Chapter 1: Hand Care	**Chapter 2: Foot Care**	**Chapter 3: Brain Care**
manicures	cleansing	wearing helmets
cleansing	trimming toenails	mental exercise
	buying properly fitting shoes	healthy input

3. Invite each child in the group to write some healthy suggestions for one aspect of care for his or her body and draw a picture to illustrate it.
4. Combine all the pages together to make a class *Body Owner's Manual.*

Taking It Further . . .

Challenge students to write a paragraph describing a body part. Invite volunteers to read their descriptions aloud and encourage other students to guess what body parts are being described.

Here Are My Hands

• BIONIC BODY •

Materials:

- lined paper
- drawing paper
- pencils

Lesson Procedure

1. Compare different parts of the body to mechanical and electronic equipment. Discuss how body parts and machines can sometimes accomplish similar tasks.

   hand—crane
   foot—wheel
   brain—computer
   eye—camera
   ear—receiver
   mouth—microphone
   teeth—blender

2. Invite each student to draw a picture of a machine on drawing paper. Have students label the pictures and then tell what body parts the functions most closely resemble. For example, a student might draw a picture of a computer and tell that its function closely resembles the function of a brain.
3. Encourage students to use lined paper to explain the connection between the machine and the body part.

Taking It Further . . .

Invite students to cut out and match magazine pictures of machines and body parts. Bring in actual models of machines and equipment to demonstrate how they work.

Here Are My Hands

ME ART

Materials:

- butcher paper
- construction paper
- glue
- scissors
- paper towels
- tempera paint
- aluminum foil
- yarn (in assorted hair colors)
- buttons

Lesson Procedure

1. With adult assistance and supervision, invite each child to make a life-size replica of his or her body. This art project is best done in several sessions and may take three or four days to complete.
2. Begin by tracing the outline of each student's body on butcher paper. Parent volunteers can help do the tracing, or children can work in pairs and trace one another. Have children cut out their body tracings.
3. Use aluminum foil to make an impression of each student's nose. Students can glue their foil noses to the heads on their body tracings.
4. Have each student bring two buttons from home to use as eyes. Encourage students to choose buttons that most closely resemble their own eyes. Students glue the buttons to the heads on their body tracings.
5. Have students glue yarn (the color that most closely matches their own hair color) around the head for hair. Invite students to decorate their paper bodies in other ways as well, such as adding feet, hands, clothing, and so on.

Taking It Further . . .

Invite students to write descriptive paragraphs about themselves on 4" x 6" cards. Attach the cards to the bottom of each body picture.

Knots on a

In this poignant story, Grandfather tells his grandson a story he loves to hear again and again—the story of a young Indian boy and the events that surrounded his birth. Through this conversation, the reader learns about courage, hope, and love. The story deals sensitively with the young boy's blindness, his increasing self-confidence, and his family's love and encouragement.

Written by Bill Martin, Jr., and
John Archambault
Illustrated by Ted Rand
New York: Henry Holt, 1987

Counting Rope

• MEMORIZING POETRY •

Materials:

•rope or twine (one yard for each student)
•10-15 poems (4-8 lines copied on 3" x 5" cards)

Lesson Procedure

1. Remind students how Grandfather tied a knot in the counting rope each time the story was told. He told the boy that when the rope was filled with knots, he would know the story by heart and could tell it himself.
2. Divide the class into groups of 4-6 students. Explain that each group will learn a poem just as the boy learned his story—with a counting rope. Give each group a one-yard length of rope or twine to use as a counting rope.
3. Ask a member of each group to select one of the short poems written on 3" x 5" cards. Invite each group to designate one member as the "reader." After the reader has read the poem one time, invite the rest of the group to read the poem together. The reader then reads the poem again and encourages the group members to repeat as much of the poem as possible from memory. The poem is read as many times as necessary until the group feels comfortable reciting the poem from memory.
4. *Each* time the poem is read, the students tie *another* knot in their counting ropes.
5. When the counting ropes are full of knots, invite each group to recite their poems in front of the class. If a group shows some uncertainty, look at their ropes and remind them that they still have room for a few more knots. Give the group a few more minutes to practice.

Taking It Further . . .

Discuss student reactions to this method of memorization. Students who are visual learners will probably express some frustration. Many students will be surprised at their success using the counting rope. Try the same method for memorizing multiplication facts.

CREATING VISUAL IMAGES

Materials:

•lined paper
•pencils

Lesson Procedure

1. Discuss how Grandfather helped the boy to understand the concept *blue* even though the boy had never seen the color. Grandfather described blue as morning, sunrise, the sky as soft as lamb's wool, and the song of birds.
2. Encourage students to think about how they would describe a familiar sight to someone who had never seen it before.
3. Choose an item and invite students to help you write a descriptive paragraph about it. We rely heavily on our sense of sight for descriptions. However, remind students that they are describing the item to someone who cannot see and can therefore not use information gathered from their sense of sight in the description. Some suggestions are:

a tree	the ocean	a race car
a painting	a bird in flight	a butterfly

4. Invite each student to choose an item and write a descriptive paragraph that would create a visual image for a person who could not see.

Taking It Further . . .

Repeat the same activity eliminating a different sense in the description. For example, invite students to describe, in writing, a dog's bark or laughter for someone who could not hear.

❧ • BIRTH STORY • ❧

Materials:

•lined paper
•pencils

Lesson Procedure

1. Remind the students how the story begins with the dramatic account of the boy's birth. Encourage students to share any information they know about their birth stories. Encourage children to share adoption stories as well.

2. Assign students the task of researching to find out more information involving their births or adoptions. Encourage students to ask parents and relatives for information.

3. After information has been collected, invite students to write their own birth stories. Point out how the story in *Knots on a Counting Rope* is told in dialog. Encourage students to think about point-of-view and writing style when writing their birth stories.

Taking It Further . . .

Compare student birth stories. Make a graph showing what months the births took place. Or, insert a pushpin in a United States or world map to indicate where each student was born.

• GALLOP COUNT •

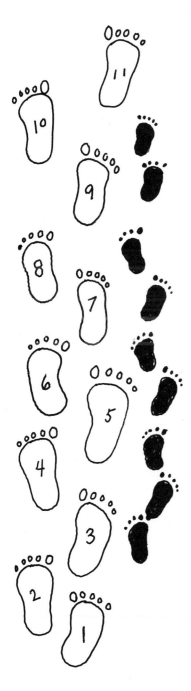

Materials:

- lined paper
- pencils

Lesson Procedure

1. Remind children how the young Indian boy learned from his horse, Rainbow, when to turn by counting her gallops.
2. Measure some classroom distances by counting the steps it takes to go from one place to another. Ask a student to walk from his or her desk to the pencil sharpener. Invite the rest of the class to count the number of steps and the turns the student takes. For example, the student might take three steps forward, two steps to the left, and then four steps forward.
3. With partners, invite students to count and record paths to the playground, library, or cafeteria. One partner walks the path while the other partner counts the steps and writes them down. After the directions are written down, students can read the directions and lead their partners to the proper destinations.

Taking It Further . . .

Invite students to count and write down the steps for some familiar pathways at home, such as from their rooms to the refrigerator!

• MATH DRILL •

Materials:

- •butcher paper
- •3" x 5" cards
- •markers or crayons
- •scissors
- •pushpins

Lesson Procedure

1. Discuss the horse race in which the boy raced his horse, Rainbow, with all his heart. Show children the picture from the book of the horses galloping across the dusty plain.
2. Divide the class into teams of 6-8 students for a horse race math drill. Give each team a 3" x 5" card and markers or crayons to draw a racehorse.
3. Design a racetrack on butcher paper. Make about 10-20 spaces from the starting line to the finish.
4. Have each team pin its racehorse to the starting line with a pushpin.
5. Line teams up single file, facing the front of the room. The first player in each line competes to answer a flashcard, math story problem, or mental math problem. The team that is first to answer the problem correctly can move its horse one space. After each problem, the head player in each line moves to the back of the line and the next players move forward to answer a question. Continue playing until one team's horse reaches the finish line.

Taking It Further . . .

Have a language arts, science, or social studies horse race. Ask questions from any unit of study to provide reinforcement and review.

• DARK MOUNTAINS •

Materials

•rope or twine (one-yard length for each student)

Lesson Procedure

1. Discuss how the term "dark mountains" was used in the story.
2. Give each child a one-yard length of rope or twine.
3. Encourage children to think of difficult times in their lives. Some children may think of major "dark mountains," such as divorce, death of a loved one, or moving away from friends. Other students may think of smaller difficult times, such as taking a math test or playing a challenging game.
4. Invite each student to tie a knot in his or her counting rope to represent each "dark mountain."
5. After giving students enough time to reflect, ask for volunteers to share one of their "dark mountain" experiences. Students may realize, as others share, that they are not alone in facing problems. Students will also be able to empathize with their classmates.

Taking It Further . . .

Suggest that students keep their counting ropes at home as reminders of the courage they have already shown. The knotted rope can be an encouragement when they face the next "dark mountain" experience.

❧ • NAMING CEREMONY • ❧

Materials:

•lined paper
•pencils
•book of names and their meanings

Lesson Procedure

1. Discuss the naming ceremony in the story in which Grandfather named the boy "Boy-Strength-of-Blue-Horses." He was given this name because the name signified strength.
2. Invite students to research the meaning and significance of their own names and give a report at a special naming ceremony. Each report should include the student's name, its meaning, any anecdotes about why the name was chosen, and a baby picture.
3. Give children an opportunity to share their reports on a specially assigned day.

Taking It Further . . .

Encourage students to invite parents and grandparents to the naming ceremony when the reports are shared. Students might also enjoy choosing a new name for themselves based on a particular quality or characteristic they admire.

Listen to the

The music of the rain is eloquently captured in this tone poem—from the soft overture of raindrops to the crescendo of a storm and then to the gentle finale and silence. Exquisite illustrations add to the drama of this word symphony.

Written by Bill Martin, Jr., and
John Archambault
Illustrated by James Endicott
New York: Henry Holt, 1988

Rain

RAIN POEM

Materials:

- lined paper
- pencils
- the record "Mississippi Suite" by Ferde Grofé

Lesson Procedure

1. Reread the book very slowly and invite the class to help compile a list of words used in the story to describe the rain. Write the list on the chalkboard.
2. Ask students to then categorize the words into three groups—words that describe soft rain, words that describe medium rain, and words that describe hard rain.

Soft Rain	Medium Rain	Hard Rain
whisper	singing	roaring
sprinkle	tiptoe	pouring
drip-drop	pitter-patter	hurly-burly
tinkle	splish	topsy-turvy
	splash	lashing
	splatter	gnashing

3. Discuss the three lists of words. Invite children to add other "rain" words to the lists as well.
4. Play the record "Mississippi Suite" for the children. Encourage students to use the words from the lists to write original rain poems while they listen to the inspiring music.

Taking It Further . . .

Invite each student to cut a large raindrop from blue construction paper. Have students mount their poems in the center of the raindrops. Display the raindrops on a bulletin board entitled "The Sounds of Rain." Encourage students to add ducks, butterflies, flowers, and puddles to the display.

• RAIN CHOIR •

Materials:

•worksheet on page 64

Lesson Procedure

1. Give each student a copy of the worksheet on page 64.
2. Divide the class into three groups. Have each group stand in a different section of the classroom.
3. Orchestrate the reading of the poem by pointing to each group when it is their turn to read in unison.

   Group 1: "Listen to the rain,"
   Group 2: "the whisper of the rain,"

   Group 1: "the slow soft sprinkle,"
   Group 2: "the drip-drop tinkle,"
   Group 3: "the first wet whisper of the rain."

4. Invite children to reread the poem together. This time, have the first group read the section about the soft rain. Have the first and second groups read the section about the medium, splish-splash rain. Have all three groups read the section about the hard rain. Then have only the third group read the last section about the quietude of the rain.

Taking It Further . . .

Paul Fleischman's *Joyful Noise* is an excellent source of poems for two voices. Encourage children to read the poems with a partner.

Name _____

Listen to the Rain

Listen to the rain,
the whisper of the rain,
the slow soft sprinkle,
the drip-drop tinkle,
the first wet whisper of
the rain.

Listen to the rain,
the singing of the rain,
the tiptoe pitter-patter,
the splish and splash
and splatter,
the steady sound,
the singing of the rain.

Listen to the rain,
the roaring pouring rain,
the hurly-burly
topsy-turvy
lashing gnashing teeth of
rain,
the lightning-flashing

thunder-crashing
sounding pounding roar-
ing rain,
leaving all outdoors a
muddle,
a mishy mushy muddy
puddle.

Listen to the quietude,
the silence and the solitude
of after-rain,
the dripping, dripping,
dropping,
the slowly, slowly stopping
the fresh
wet
silent
after-time
of rain.

Reprinted from *Listen to the Rain* with permission of the authors,
Bill Martin, Jr., and John Archambault.

The Bill Martin, Jr., Connection © 1991 Fearon Teacher Aids

• RAIN MAP •

Materials:

- •worksheet on page 66
- •encyclopedias or social studies texts
- •colored pencils or crayons

Lesson Procedure

1. Encourage students to use resource books, such as encyclopedias or textbooks, to determine areas in the world that have the greatest and least amounts of precipitation.
2. Give each student a copy of the world map worksheet. Invite each student to color the world map to indicate the amount of precipitation in various parts of the world. Students can color the areas of high precipitation green, the moderate areas yellow, and the areas with very little precipitation brown.
3. Have students make a color key to explain what each color on the map represents.

Taking It Further . . .

Challenge students to make a precipitation map of their own state. Compare your community's annual rainfall with the rainfall of other communities in your state.

Name _____

World Rainfall

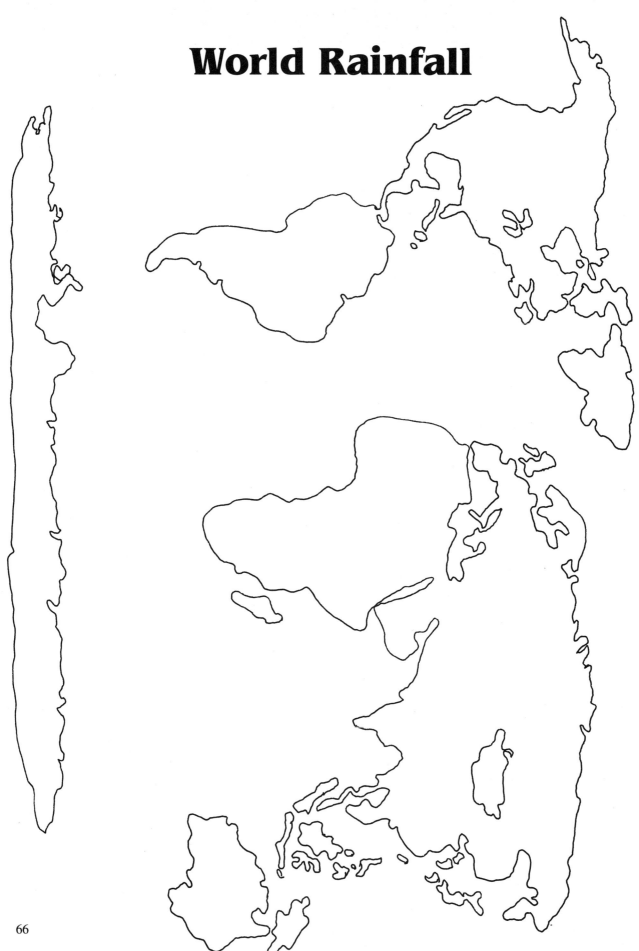

BUTTERFLY ART

Materials:

- worksheet on page 68
- pictures of butterflies
- watercolor paint and brushes
- black markers or crayons
- scissors

Lesson Procedure

1. Point out the beautiful butterfly in the story. Show children other pictures of butterflies.
2. Discuss the many patterns and colors that can be found on a butterfly's wings.
3. Give each student a copy of the worksheet and invite children to paint one-half of the butterfly in order to create a beautiful design.
4. Have children fold the paper in half on the dotted line while the paint is still wet to transfer the design to the other side of the butterfly. Open the designs and allow them to dry.
5. After the paint is dry, children can use a black marker or crayon to draw the outline on the other side of the butterfly.
6. Invite children to cut the butterflies out and display them on a bulletin board. Discuss the symmetry of the butterflies.

Taking It Further . . .

Children can make beautiful handprint butterflies. Students dip one hand in a shallow dish of tempera paint, then press their hands on one side of a sheet of paper. Have students fold their papers in half to transfer the handprints to the other side. Open the papers and let the handprint butterflies dry. Children can then cut out the butterflies.

Name _____

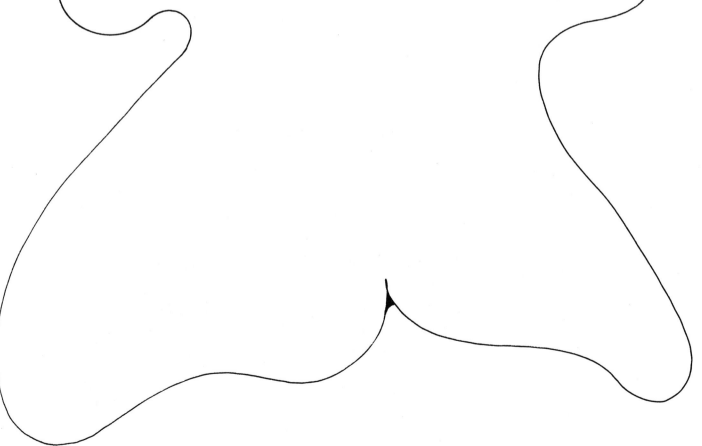

Listen to the Rain

The Bill Martin, Jr., Connection © 1991 Fearon Teacher Aids

The Magic

Is it foolery? Or is it just the bedeviled imagination of a storyteller on Halloween night? Are they really foolies or are they just the neighborhood trick-or-treaters? This story is as full of magic and mischief as the authors themselves.

Written by Bill Martin, Jr., and
John Archambault
Illustrated by Robert J. Lee
New York: Henry Holt, 1989

Pumpkin

❧• PUMPKIN PICKING •❧

Materials:

- worksheet on page 71
- pencils

Lesson Procedure

1. Remind children that the storyteller chose what he thought was the perfect pumpkin. Ask students what criteria they would have used for choosing a perfect pumpkin.
2. Invite students to make a list of rules or guidelines on the worksheet for choosing the perfect pumpkin. Remind students to use complete sentences. Students can include how they would carve their pumpkins into perfect jack-o'-lanterns as well.

Taking It Further . . .

Read *Everybody Needs a Rock* by Byrd Baylor (New York: Scribner, 1974). Invite children to compare their thoughts about choosing the perfect pumpkin to criteria used for choosing the perfect rock.

The Magic Pumpkin

Pumpkin Picking

_____
_____
_____
_____
_____
_____
_____
_____
_____
_____
_____
_____
_____
_____
_____
_____
_____
_____
_____
_____
_____
_____

❧ • VOCABULARY • ☙

Materials:

- worksheet on page 73
- pencils
- scissors
- dictionaries

Lesson Procedure

1. Reread the story and pause at unfamiliar words or phrases to discuss their meanings. For example, ask students why they think the author referred to the pumpkin as "a royal prince of seed and vine." Discuss the meaning of such words as *stupefied, phantom, shamelessly,* and *surging.*
2. Give pairs of children a worksheet and invite them to use a dictionary to write a definition for each word.
3. Have children cut the word cards apart.
4. Children can use the word cards to challenge each other in a vocabulary game. One student reads the definition aloud while the partner tries to name the word that is defined. If the student answers correctly, he or she keeps the card. If the answer is not correct, the reader keeps the card. When all the cards have been read, players switch roles.

Taking It Further . . .

Challenge students to use the words in original sentences. Check the sentences for accuracy. Invite volunteers to read their best sentences aloud to the class, but leave out the vocabulary word. The volunteer can choose a classmate to fill in the missing word.

The Magic Pumpkin

tomfoolery	mystic	glare
_____	_____	_____
_____	_____	_____
_____	_____	_____
_____	_____	_____
_____	_____	_____

dreadful	phantom	sneer
_____	_____	_____
_____	_____	_____
_____	_____	_____
_____	_____	_____
_____	_____	_____

stupefy	shameless	turncoat
_____	_____	_____
_____	_____	_____
_____	_____	_____
_____	_____	_____

mischief	surge	wither
_____	_____	_____
_____	_____	_____
_____	_____	_____
_____	_____	_____

The Bill Martin, Jr., Connection © 1991 Fearon Teacher Aids

• MATH FOOLIES •

Materials:

- worksheet on page 75
- pencils
- toothpicks

Lesson Procedure

1. Give each child a copy of the worksheet.
2. Divide the class into groups of 3-4 to solve the math brainteasers. Ask students to draw pictures and use toothpicks to create visual images to help solve the problems.
3. After students have worked out an answer for each problem, share solutions and the processes students used to arrive at the answers.

Answers to Worksheet

1. First, take the foolie to the porch because it is safe to leave the witch and the treats alone in the pumpkin patch. Then, take the witch to the porch and take the foolie back with you to the pumpkin patch. Leaving the foolie in the pumpkin patch, take the treats and leave them on the porch with the witch. Return to the pumpkin patch and bring the foolie to the porch.
2. To make three squares, you would need to move only two sticks.
   To make two squares, you would need to move only four sticks.
   To make one square, you would need to move only four sticks.
3. If you started with one foolie, in ten minutes there would be 2 foolies.

   20 minutes=4 foolies   40 minutes=16 foolies   60 minutes=64 foolies
   30 minutes=8 foolies   50 minutes=32 foolies

4. Together, Pumpkin A and Pumpkin B roll 25 feet every second. One hundred can be divided by 25 four times. So it will take the pumpkins four seconds to meet at the bottom of the hills. In four seconds, Pumpkin A will roll 40 feet, so that hill is 40 feet high. In four seconds, Pumpkin B will roll 60 feet, so that hill is 60 feet high.

Taking It Further . . .

Encourage students to create their own math foolies. Children can look through brainteaser math books and adapt the problems using a Halloween theme.

Math Foolies

1. There is a witch, a foolie, and a bag of treats sitting in a pumpkin patch. You need to take all three to your front porch, but you can only take one at a time. The problem is, the witch can never be left alone with the foolie because she might turn the foolie into a frog. And, the foolie can never be left alone with the treats because he will eat them. How can you move everything to your porch, one at a time, without any problems?

2. A band of foolies dropped 12 drumsticks in the yard in the pattern shown.

   What is the smallest number of drumsticks you would have to move to change the pattern into 3 squares? _____

   What is the smallest number of drumsticks you would have to move to change the original pattern into 2 squares? _____

   What is the smallest number of drumsticks you would have to move to change the original pattern into 1 square? _____

3. If a foolie were able to double himself every ten minutes, how many foolies would there be in one hour?_____

4. Two pumpkins start rolling down two hills toward each other.

   The hilltops are 100 feet apart, but they are different heights. Pumpkin A rolls 10 feet every second. Pumpkin B rolls 15 feet every second. Both pumpkins will reach the bottom of their hills at the same time. How long will it take the two pumpkins to meet at the bottom? _____

   How tall is the hill Pumpkin A rolled down? _____
   How tall is the hill Pumpkin B rolled down? _____

Materials:

- worksheet on page 77
- pumpkin seeds
- pencils
- math flashcards

Lesson Procedure

1. Give each child a bingo worksheet and 16 pumpkin seeds.
2. Have students randomly write one number between 0 and 20 in each square on their bingo cards to practice addition or subtraction facts. Or, write a multiplication-product chart on the board and have older students randomly copy one number in each square on the bingo card to practice multiplication facts.
3. Use flashcards to present appropriate math problems (addition, subtraction, or multiplication).
4. If students have the answer to the problem on their bingo cards, they cover the square with a pumpkin seed.
5. The first student to cover four squares in a horizontal, vertical, or diagonal row calls "Bingo." If the player's answers coincide with the answers for the cards that have been presented, the student wins.

Taking It Further . . .

Play pumpkin seed Bingo for vocabulary review. Have students randomly write a vocabulary word from a selected list in each square on their cards. Read the word definitions. Students cover the square that contains the word for each definition as it is read.

Name _____

❧ • JACK-O'-LANTERN ART • ☙

Materials:

- orange construction paper
- yellow tissue paper
- pencils
- crayons or markers
- scissors
- glue

Lesson Procedure

1. Give each child a large piece of orange construction paper and invite children to draw a jack-o'-lantern's face with pencil.
2. Encourage children to add details to the jack-o'-lanterns with crayons or markers.
3. Have children cut out the eyes, nose, and mouth.
4. Children can glue a sheet of yellow tissue paper to the back of their jack-o'-lanterns to create the illusion of a candle's glow from inside the pumpkin.
5. Hang the jack-o'-lanterns in the window to catch the sunlight and enhance the effect.

Taking It Further . . .

Make mini-jack-o'-lanterns using blown eggshells. Or make maxi-jack-o'-lanterns using a variety of materials. Divide the class into groups of four. Provide laundry baskets, covered boxes, orange socks, newspapers, felt, orange balloons, tape, and string. Watch the young inventors go to work!

Up and Down

The story's cadence catches up with the mood as the merry-go-round whirls and spins. The burst of joy comes to an end as the merry-go-round slowly winds down. The bright illustrations follow the pace of the merry-go-round adding excitement and wonder to the story.

Written by Bill Martin, Jr., and
John Archambault
Illustrated by Ted Rand
New York: Henry Holt, 1985

on the Merry-Go-Round

❧ • CREATIVE WRITING • ❧

Materials:

- •worksheet on page 81
- •pencils

Lesson Procedure

1. The child in the story enjoyed the feeling of galloping wild and free on a painted pony. Encourage children to share their similar experiences.
2. Invite children to imagine the thrill of actually galloping *off* the carousel on the painted pony and embarking on an imaginary adventure.
3. Ask students to imagine what their carousel horse would look like, where they would go on their painted ponies, and what would happen along the way.
4. Give each student a worksheet and invite children to create a story using their own ideas.

Taking It Further . . .

Read *Carousel* by Donald Crews (Greenwillow Books, 1982). Encourage children to notice how the impression of movement is created through special photography of his illustrations.

Up and Down on the Merry-Go-Round

Name _____

The Painted Pony Adventure

_____
_____
_____
_____
_____
_____
_____

_____
_____
_____
_____
_____
_____
_____
_____
_____
_____
_____

• VOCABULARY •

Materials:

•lined paper
•pencils

Lesson Procedure

1. The authors used carefully chosen descriptive words to create the pace of the story.
2. Discuss the words and phrases the authors chose to create the sensation of speed.

   flying mane
   wild and free
   dizzy
   galloping
   whirling
   horse with wings
   ride the wind

3. The pace of the story winds down and comes to a halt just as the merry-go-round slows to a stop. Discuss the ways in which the authors used words and phrases to convey this feeling.

   winking
   bells a-tinkling
   slowing
   m e r r y g o o o o r o o o o u u u n d

4. Encourage students to make their own lists of words that create images of speed or stillness.

Taking It Further . . .

Children can use their word lists in writing stories or poems.

• MONEY •

Materials:

•worksheet on page 84
•pencils

Lesson Procedure

1. Look again at the illustrations in the story. Ask children to identify some things that could be purchased at a carnival or fair and to add some of their own ideas.

   balloons   soft drinks
   merry-go-round tickets   cotton candy
   popcorn   souvenirs

2. Give each student a copy of the worksheet and invite children to calculate the cost of a day at the carnival.

   Answers to Worksheet
   1. 10 rides
   2. $1.50
   3. $5.00
   4. $4.00
   5. 4 tickets left
   6. $7.00
   7. answers will vary

Taking It Further . . .

Plan a classroom carnival. Design simple arcade games, such as throwing a ball through a hoola hoop. Open a concession stand to sell popcorn and lemonade. Give students play money or tickets and invite them to enjoy the carnival and spend their "money" wisely!

Name _____

One for the Money

Use the prices listed on the carnival sign to solve each problem.

balloon $1.50
ride ticket   50¢
popcorn $1.00
drink   75¢
cotton candy $1.25
souvenir $2.50

1. Marcy has $5.00. She plans to spend her whole day at the carnival riding the carousel. How many times will she be able to ride it before she runs out of money? _____

2. Mark also has $5.00. He plans to ride the carousel twice, buy a balloon and some popcorn, and save the rest of the money. How much money will Mark save? _____

3. Jenna has enough money to buy three carousel rides, two boxes of popcorn, and one cotton candy. At the end of the day, she will have only 25¢ left. How much money did Jenna have at the beginning of the day? _____

4. Kyle and Alan each want a balloon. They also want to ride the carousel once each. How much money will they need? _____

5. Rita bought 20 ride tickets. She gave 5 tickets to her brother, 3 tickets to her younger sister, and she used 8 tickets herself. She decided to save the tickets she had left. How many tickets did Rita save? _____

6. If Michelle buys one of everything at the carnival, except a ride ticket, how much money will she need? _____

7. If you had $5.00 to spend at the carnival, what would you buy?_____ How much money would you have left? _____

The Bill Martin, Jr., Connection © 1991 Fearon Teacher Aids

Up and Down on the Merry-Go-Round

✦ CAROUSEL CONTRAPTION ✦

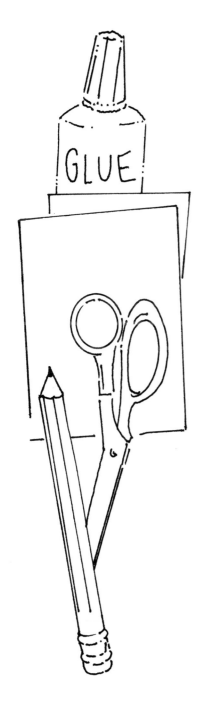

Materials:

- worksheet on page 86
- crayons or markers
- tagboard
- scissors
- glue

Lesson Procedure

1. Give each child a carousel worksheet and invite students to color it with bright colors.
2. Have students glue the carousel to a piece of tagboard and then carefully cut around it.
3. Discuss ways students could make their carousels spin and whirl as the one in the story seemed to do.

   Twirl it.
   Insert a pencil through the center and spin it.
   Make it into a pinwheel.
   Roll it down an inclined plane.

4. In small groups of 2-4 children, invite students to experiment with various methods of carousel propulsion, incorporating what they know about simple machines.

Taking It Further . . .

Challenge students to work with someone at home to make models of carnival rides with moving parts.

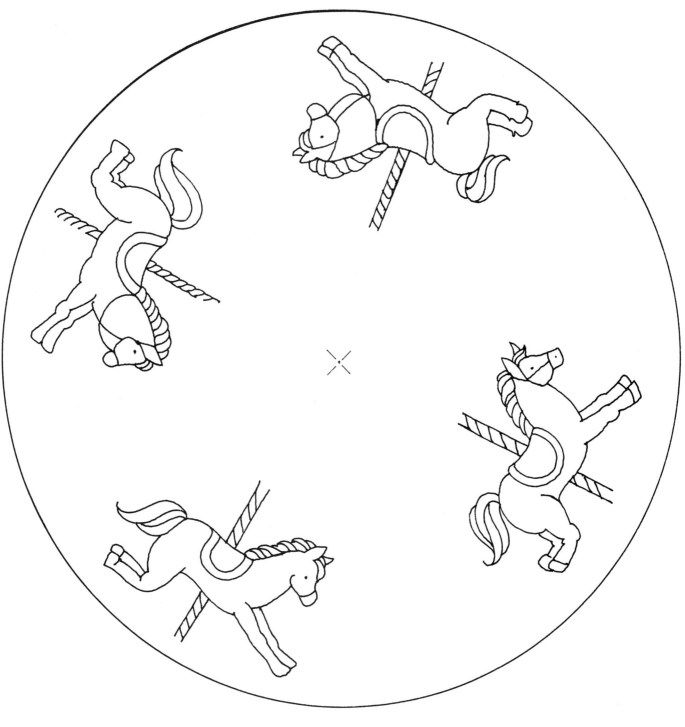

Up and Down on the Merry-Go-Round

The Bill Martin, Jr., Connection © 1991 Fearon Teacher Aids

 • FOOD CHAINS •

Materials:

- adding-machine tape
- crayons or markers
- pencils
- tape

Lesson Procedure

1. Remind children of the circular motion of the carousel and how the child riding it passed by the same sights with each revolution.
2. Explain to children that there are cycles in nature that repeat themselves, just as the cycle of the carousel repeated itself over and over again. Encourage children to name some cycles in nature (seasons of the year, water cycle).
3. Discuss the cycle of an ecosystem-food chain. In each ecosystem, the sun provides energy that *primary producers* need to make food. Primary producers are mainly green plants, such as grass and trees. *Primary consumers,* such as mice, rabbits, grasshoppers, and other plant-eating animals, feed on the primary producers. Foxes, skunks, and other *secondary consumers* feed on animals. *Decomposers* (bacteria, fungi) break down dead plants and animals into simple nutrients that go back into the soil.
4. Give each student a strip of adding-machine tape on which to illustrate a food chain.
5. Invite children to tape the ends of the strips together to make circular loops.

Taking It Further . . .

Encourage students to do some research on how people are affecting nature's cycles. Invite students to report on ways people are interfering with or helping nature's delicate balance.

• MOBILES •

Materials:

- •worksheet on page 89
- •wire coat hangers
- •string
- •thread
- •9" x 12" construction paper (variety of colors)
- •pencils
- •crayons or markers
- •plastic drinking straws
- •glue
- •scissors
- •needle or pin
- •box cutter or exacto knife

Lesson Procedure

1. Invite students to cut out the worksheet pattern on page 89 and trace around it on colored construction paper. Encourage students to round corners and add details to personalize the carousel horses.
2. Have students cut out the construction-paper horses. Invite students to decorate both sides of the carousel horses.
3. The teacher or adult volunteer cuts a 3" slit in the middle of the straw for each horse. Invite students to insert horses through the slits in the straws.
4. Poke a hole through the top end of the straw with a needle or pin and thread a piece of string through the hole.
5. For each group of four students, bend a wire coat hanger into a circle. Hang the coat hanger ring from the ceiling with four strings. Hang four horses from each hanger.

Taking It Further . . .

Encourage students to write short poems about their carousel horses on 3" x 5" cards. Hang the cards along with the horses on the mobiles.

Up and Down on the Merry-Go-Round

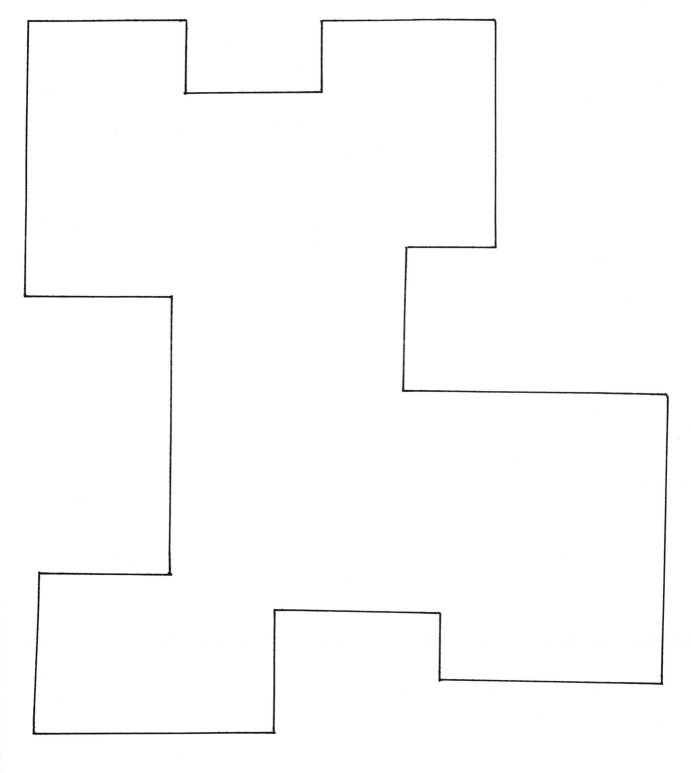

Up and Down on the Merry-Go-Round

White Dynamite and

White Dynamite is the meanest bull in the whole United States. But Curly Kidd is the best bull rider. The story, told in rapid dialog, is action-packed and full of rodeo atmosphere, fittingly illustrated with Ted Rand's dusty paintings.

Written by Bill Martin, Jr., and
John Archambault
Illustrated by Ted Rand
New York: Henry Holt, 1986

Curly Kidd

❧ RODEO VOCABULARY ❧

Materials:

•lined paper
•pencils
•dictionaries and encyclopedias

Lesson Procedure

1. Discuss the meaning of some of the rodeo terms used in the book, such as *chute*, *pitchin'*, and *bull rider*.
2. Invite children to share any knowledge they have about rodeo events. Explain to children that bull riding is considered the most dangerous of the rodeo events. A rider attempts to stay on a bull for eight seconds.
3. Point out the clowns in the illustrations throughout the story. Explain that the rodeo clowns help distract the bull if the rider should fall off while the rider tries to get safely out of the area.
4. Write the following list of rodeo terms on the chalkboard. Invite children to use dictionaries and encyclopedias to define the terms.

1. blow a stirrup—to let a foot come out of the stirrup
2. break—to train a horse
3. bronco—wild, untamed horse
4. buck—to spring into the air with the back arched
5. bulldogging—steer wrestling
6. dogie—a motherless calf in a range herd
7. lariat—a long rope with a noose used to catch livestock
8. lasso—to rope horses or cattle
9. picking daisies—describes a rider who has been thrown
10. scratching—spurring a steer's shoulders to make it buck
11. spur—pointed device attached to a cowboy's boot
12. stetson— a broad-brimmed felt hat
13. tenderfoot—a beginner

Taking It Further . . .

Encourage students to research other rodeo events, such as saddle-bronc riding, calf roping, and steer dogging.

White Dynamite and Curly Kidd

☙• SADDLE UP •❧

Materials:

•worksheet on page 94
•pencils
•crayons or markers

Lesson Procedure

1. Point out the illustration of the saddle hanging on a fence near the end of the story.
2. Give each student a copy of the worksheet and write the terms used to label the saddle parts on the chalkboard.

cantle
skirt
flank strap
saddle horn
saddle jockey
tie strap
stirrup
seat

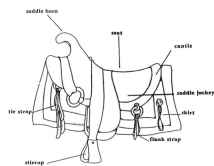

3. Discuss each term and help students match the proper terms to the saddle parts on their worksheets.
4. Encourage students to color their worksheets when they are finished.

Taking It Further . . .

Challenge students to draw diagrams of horses and label the parts. Students might also enjoy labeling a cowboy's or cowgirl's outfit.

Name _____

Saddle Up

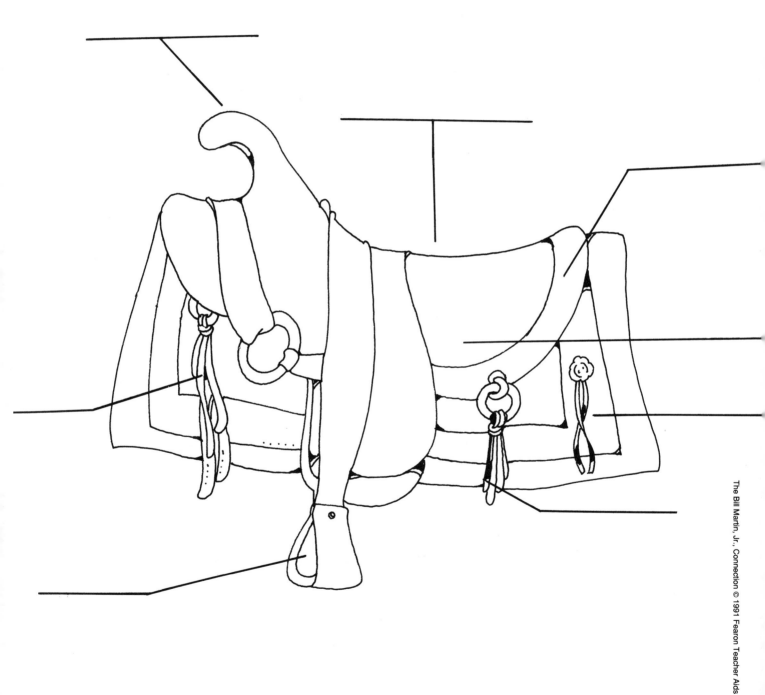

The Bill Martin, Jr., Connection © 1991 Fearon Teacher Aids

White Dynamite and Curly Kidd

• CAREERS •

Materials:

- •lined paper
- •pencils
- •resource books on careers

Lesson Procedure

1. Lucky wanted to be a rodeo rider just like her father, Curly Kidd. Encourage students to share what they would like to be or do when they grow up.
2. Lucky was learning some requirements for being a rodeo rider by watching her father. Encourage students to consider what skills would be essential for their career choices.
3. Give each student a sheet of lined paper. Invite children to write down their career choices and to use the resource books to list some necessary qualifications for the job.

Taking It Further . . .

Challenge students to write stories about their chosen careers. For example, write a story about the first day on the job. Encourage students to use their imaginations as they write about their futures.

❦ • HANDLING FEAR • ❧

Materials:

•lined paper
•pencils

Lesson Procedure

1. Discuss how Lucky, like her father, chewed gum and recite names of places to keep from being frightened as she rode.
2. Discuss other methods that people use to instill bravery and ward off fear.

   whistle
   think of friends
   sing

3. Invite children to list ways they have tried or would advise someone to try to overcome feelings of fear.
4. Invite children to share helpful ideas as a means of encouraging others. Help children realize that everyone has fears and they are not alone.

Taking It Further . . .

Invite children to design their own rodeo posters advertising courage.

THE
Bill Martin, Jr.,
CONNECTION

By Will C. Howell

The Bill Martin, Jr., Connection is written for teachers and librarians who want to effectively use good literature in their classrooms. The variety of activities, which are geared to meet the needs of students from first grade to sixth grade, require minimal preparation, while resulting in maximum participation and learning.

Your students can be amateur detectives using handprints for clues, participate in indoor rainstorms using choral reading, and play Pumpkin Bingo while practicing math skills.

But most important, they will develop an ability to compare, analyze, and enjoy a single author's literary and artistic style. Stimulate your students to become more involved in and enthusiastic about reading, writing, and learning by "connecting" with this outstanding author.

For a complete catalog, write:

Fearon Teacher Aids

PO Box 280

Carthage, Illinois 62321

ISBN 0-86653-991-3